GARFIELD
THE ME BOOK

A Guide To Superiority:
How To Get It, Use It, And Keep It

Created by JIM DAVIS

Text by Jim Kraft
Illustrations by Brett Koth
Design by Betsy Brackett
Art Support by Kevin Campbell, Kimberly Conway, Larry Fentz, Thomas Howard, Lynette Nuding

BALLANTINE BOOKS • NEW YORK

 Published in the United States by Ballantine Books, a division of Random House, Inc., New York, and simultaneously in Canada by Random House of Canada Limited, Toronto.

Library of Congress Catalog Card Number: 89-91788

ISBN: 0-345-36545-3

Manufactured in the United States of America

First Edition: April 1990

10 9 8 7 6 5 4 3 2 1

CONTENTS

A little ego goes nowhere.

Garfield

INTRODUCTION

According to my mother, I weighed five pounds, six ounces at birth, and two pounds of that was ego. Personally, I think it was more like four pounds.

From the very beginning I had a keen sense of who and what really mattered in my life. All the other kittens on my block said "meow"; I preferred "me first." Obviously, I was destined for greatness. I mean, all I had to do was look in the mirror. No way was Mother Nature going to waste that kind of charisma on a common mouser!

Well, some of us are just born superior. If you aren't one of the lucky few, however, there's no need to be discouraged. Anyone can become

a superior person, provided they are willing to give of themselves to themselves. That's what this book is all about. First of all, it will teach you to stop putting so much emphasis on the opinions of others, and start listening to the one person who really knows what's best for you . . . namely, me! I'll teach you how to find that ego-maniac that resides within all of us and bring it to the surface, where it can scream for the attention it deserves. Then, once your ego has been sufficiently inflated, I'll show you how to put it to work. Follow my advice and you'll soon have a superiority complex that will be the envy (or possibly the end) of all your friends.

Starting right now, decide that *you* are going to be the most important person in your life. Go ahead! You'll thank yourself for it later. ❦

· CHAPTER ONE ·

TRIPPING THROUGH THE EGO

•ME•

The road to superiority begins at the ego. And when it comes to big egos, I wrote the book. In fact, I wrote *this* book.

"Ego," as any ancient Roman knows, is the Latin word for "I." This means that the concept of an individual self is very old. When a Roman said, "I really hate it when the Huns drop in," he knew that he was expressing his own individual feelings, rather than those of his neighbor, Clodius the used-slave dealer. But the sense of self is very much older than the ancient Romans. The ancient Egyptians had individual names like "Ramses" and "Seti" and "Biff." Even Neanderthal man knew that he was an individual. This is shown by the fact that prehistoric cave paintings from France feature primitive graffiti such as "Zog Sherman walks on all fours" and "I really hate it when the saber-tooth tigers drop in."

But even though these ancient peoples recognized the concept of individuality, they were not aware that they had egos in our modern sense of the word. When the Romans took pride in the

fact that they had conquered virtually all of the known world, they had no idea that this feeling had anything to do with ego. They simply thought that they were "hot stuff."

The ego as we know it today is primarily the discovery of the great Sigmund Freud, father of psychoanalysis. I'm not sure of all the details, but I think the discovery probably went something like this . . .

·ME·

(Vienna, 1898. Sigmund Freud sits at his desk, reading a copy of *Oedipus Rex* and chuckling softly.)

FREUD

Ach! These Greeks kill me! Murder your father and marry your mother? Get real!

(A woman enters)

FREDA K.

Dr. Freud! I must speak with you!

FREUD

Ja, ja. You hysterical? On Tuesdays I do a special for hysterics: one full session, plus a manicure, six marks. You can't beat it.

FREDA K.

I don't think I'm hysterical. I just need to talk to someone.

FREUD

So pull up a couch.

FREDA K.

(Lies down) Dr. Freud, I've been having this dream.

FREUD

Are you naked in this dream?

FREDA K.

Oh, no. Not at all!

FREUD

(Sighs) Go on.

FREDA K.

I'm being chased through the woods by a giant bratwurst. Suddenly I fall into a deep hole. I'm falling and falling. I land on a train. The train goes faster and faster. There's a man in black on the train. He shakes a rubber chicken at me. An elephant eats my hat. Fireworks explode. A chimp in a plaid suit tries to sell me life insurance. The train stops in Berlin. I ask the conductor, "Is this Berlin?" The conductor replies, "Do I look like a cheese to you?!" A rabbi and an Irishman get on the train. I'm frantic, because I can't remember the rest of the joke. I'm just about to yodel, when I wake up.

FREUD

I see. And how long have you been having this dream?

FREDA K.

Since I was five.

FREUD

Which is when you witnessed that ugly incident involving your mama und papa, correct?

FREDA K.

What ugly incident? There was no . . . Ach du lieber! That's it! When I was five years old, I saw Papa pull a rubber chicken from his hat and snap it at Mama, who immediately fainted. That's what's been haunting me all these years!

(She leaps from couch) Thank you, Dr. Freud! Now I can lead a normal, healthy life! But how did you know that was my problem?

FREUD

I used applied reasoning based on years of intensive investigation into the interpretation of dreams within the framework of my revolutionary theory of the unconscious.

FREDA K.

What does that mean?

FREUD

It was a lucky shot.

FREDA K.

In any case, I think you are the greatest doctor in the world, and I will sing your praises to everyone I meet!

FREUD

Don't forget to mention the Tuesday special.

FREDA K.

Auf wiedersehen! *(Exits)*

FREUD

(Leaps up, raises fists in triumph) It works! Psychoanalysis works! I'm the greatest! I'm a genius! I'm a lean, mean psychoanalyzing machine!

(Curtain)

Personally, I think that dream was about needing a midnight snack. I mean, sometimes a bratwurst is just a bratwurst. But anyway, that's how Freud supposedly discovered the ego, and if you don't buy that, you can write your own book.

Freud also discovered other facets of the mind, such as the id and the superego. In addition, he was a pioneer in waiting room magazines, and is generally regarded as the first to use the clinical term "nutso." But it is his investigation into the various functions of the ego that most concerns us here. And all of those functions pale beside the central function of the

ego, which is to make us look good in our own eyes and in the eyes of the rest of the world. A healthily inflated ego is the cornerstone of personal success, for unless we have a good opinion of ourselves, we will never be able to force that opinion upon others.

WHAT'S YOUR EQ?

·ME·

Everyone has an ego of some sort. My own is robust and large enough to affect the orbits of our neighboring planets. Jon, on the other hand, has a wimpy ego with a bad complexion, wearing a sign that says "Deflate me!" Even Odie has an ego. He just doesn't have a brain. Which is actually good, because if he had a brain he would realize that he's a dog, which would be bad for his ego.

It's time now for you to gain some insight into your own personal "I" by determining your "Ego Quotient." The EQ, as it is called by egometricians, is a measure of the current size of your ego, as well as an indicator of future ego growth. To determine your EQ, simply answer the questions appearing on the following pages and total your score.

And while you're doing that, I'll do some additional research at the mirror.

THE E.Q. TEST

1. How would you describe your face?
   A. Devastatingly attractive
   B. Not likely to cause nightmares
   C. A zit with teeth
2. Which phrase best suits your body?
   A. Finely sculpted
   B. Reasonably trim
   C. Mostly beach ball

3. When you meet someone new, they usually . . .
   A. like you immediately.
   B. like you once they get to know you.
   C. like you to leave the room.
4. Which of these activities would you prefer?
   A. Completing the hostile takeover of a major corporation
   B. Acting in a local theater production
   C. Hiding under the bed
5. You are most likely to receive . . .
   A. a Nobel Prize.
   B. a bonus for your performance on the job.
   C. a fine for wimping in public.
6. If someone criticizes you, you usually . . .
   A. assume they are jealous of you.
   B. try to decide if the criticism is valid.
   C. thank them for taking the time to humiliate you.

7. What is your best quality?
   A. You have so many, it's too hard to choose.
   B. You have a keen intelligence.
   C. You have very few communicable diseases.

8. When you daydream, you imagine yourself . . .
   A. running the world.
   B. starring in a major motion picture.
   C. hiding under the bed.
9. Your biggest fault is . . .
   A. your perfection makes others feel inadequate.
   B. you don't always give yourself enough credit.
   C. whatever your mother says it is.
10. How often do you trust your own judgement?
   A. Always
   B. Sometimes
   C. Undecided

11. Which historical figure do you most admire?
    A. Attila the Hun
    B. Christopher Columbus
    C. Napoleon's barber
12. In your estimation, the best way for you to get ahead is to . . .
    A. rely on your enormous charm and talent.
    B. work hard and hope for a break.
    C. whine and beg.

13. Would you ever use unethical methods to get ahead?
    A. Only as a first resort
    B. With great reluctance
    C. Just thinking about it gives you a rash

14. Members of the opposite sex usually find you . . .
    A. irresistible.
    B. kind of cute.
    C. hiding under the bed.

15. Your idea of success is . . .
    A. gaining wealth and power.
    B. being the best person you can be.
    C. getting your shoes on the correct feet.

SCORING

Give yourself two points for each A answer, one point for each B answer, and zero points for each C answer.

25-30 WORLD-CLASS If you become a big success, you won't be at all surprised.
16-24 INFLATED With the right training, you could achieve egomania.
10-15 LIGHTWEIGHT Not bad. At least you can push the wimps around.
5-9 WEENIE You have a bright future as a doormat.
0-4 PATHETIC Pond scum has higher self-esteem than you. Where did you ever get the nerve to buy this book?

So far I'm the only respondent ever to get a perfect score. I couldn't be prouder . . . but that won't stop me from trying.

· CHAPTER THREE ·

PUMPING EGO

·ME·

As you know, I am philosophically opposed to all forms of physical exercise. I mean, if we were meant to sweat, we'd have been born with wristbands. You don't need workouts that make you feel exhausted *and* bad about yourself. You don't need leotards that expose your shortcomings. You need something that will firm and develop your sagging self-esteem. In other words, you need Garfield's MAXIMUM IMPACT EGOROBIC WORKOUT!

The Maximum Impact Egorobic Workout is the result of many years of exhaustive self-admiration by yours truly. The exercises are designed to add both mass and tone to your ego, without the loss of any precious bodily fluids. This is the perfect workout for everyone, from kids searching for a little self-confidence to ruthless CEOs hoping to keep that world-dominating edge. Do these exercises for at least ten minutes, three times per week, and you'll soon have an ego that needs a room of its own. You can even do these exercises daily, if you like. I do. It's not that I need the practice; I just look soooo good doing them!

THE MAXIMUM IMPACT EGOROBIC WORKOUT

[CAUTION: *Before undertaking any ego-building program, be sure to consult your analyst or hairdresser. If you should experience pangs of self-doubt during a workout, simply pat yourself on the back until the pangs disappear.*]

THE BASIC PUMP

Step 1: Look at your face in mirror.

Step 2: Stop gagging.

Step 3: Say something nice to your face, e.g. "Hey, good-looking!", "Whoa! Nice nose!", or "You've got jowls to die for!"

Step 4: Repeat previous steps until you start to like what you see.

THE REVERSE PUMP

Step 1: Stand with back to mirror.

Step 2: Look over shoulder.

Step 3: Say, "Nice buns!"

Step 4: Repeat until you acquire confidence or a stiff neck.

THE POWER PUMP

Step 1: Face mirror.

Step 2: Scream, "I'm the best, the best, the best! Yeeeeees!"

Step 3: Repeat until you feel a burning sensation in your ego.
WARNING: *Never attempt the Power Pump unless you have first warmed up your ego with polite self-compliments.*

THE WEIGHT LIFT

Step 1: Fix bathroom scale so that it always registers your ideal weight.

Step 2: Stand on scale.

Step 3: Say, "Jane Fonda, eat your heart out!"

Step 4: Reward yourself with a cheesecake.

THE ME BEND

Step 1: Stand with feet together.

Step 2: Take a bow.

Step 3: Say, "Thank you! Thank you! Too much, really! I love you all! Bless you! Thank you!"

Step 4: Repeat until you are too choked up to go on.

BEG EXTENSIONS

Step 1: Sit on chair, hands resting palms-down on knees.

Step 2: Keeping palm down, raise right hand six inches above right knee.

Step 3: Hold for three seconds, which is the average time it takes a grovelling flunky to kiss a hand.

Step 4: Repeat exercise with left hand. Alternate right and left hands until you feel that both hands are grovel-ready.

THE REALITY STRETCH FOR ADULTS

Step 1: Face mirror.

Step 2: Pull back facial skin until wrinkles disappear.

Step 3: Say, "You don't look a day over 20!"

Step 4: Repeat until you can do this without laughing. If problems persist, try doing this exercise in the dark.

THE EGO RIP

Step 1: Make a list of all your shortcomings.

Step 2: Grasp list firmly in both hands.

Step 3: Rip list to shreds.

Step 4: Consider yourself perfect.

As you can see, this is a pretty intense workout. When it's over, you'll need to find a way to wind down. I recommend popping bonbons while someone massages your ego.

· CHAPTER FOUR ·

MY COUTURE IS HAUTER THAN YOURS

Have you ever asked yourself why I like to kick Odie and sharpen my claws on Jon? You probably think I do it because I get some perverse pleasure out of abusing lower life forms.

I can't argue with that.

But I believe there is also a more metaphysical reason: I do it because they insult my fashion sense. I mean, take a look at Odie. (Don't look too long or your brain will start to atrophy.) He's sort of a sickly yellow. It's definitely not his color. If you or I woke up looking like that, we'd immediately dial the paramedics.

Then there's Jon. What should I say about Jon's sense of style? What should I say about a man who buys his clothes at "Geeks R Us"?

The man has absolutely no concept of proper attire. He thinks "Clearance" is the name of a designer. And then he wonders why, every time he goes out, people ask him how long the circus will be in town.

The point is, once you have whipped your ego into shape, you will want to show it off to the rest of the world. As always, the first thing the world will notice about you is the way you are dressed. Therefore, you must dress like a superior person. You must not suffocate a first-class ego in no-class clothes. Remember, clothes make a statement. And *your* wardrobe should scream, "I'm fabulous, you're so-so!"

So here are my suggestions for dressing your ego. I don't expect them to appeal to all of my readers . . . just the ones with taste.

SEVEN TIPS FOR SUPERIOR STYLE

1. Wear monogrammed clothes, but only if you have suitable initials. "GOD" is okay. "DOG" isn't. If your initials spell out a body part, consider filing a lawsuit against your parents.
2. To pump up a "weak" outfit, add superior accessories, such as a silk scarf, or a Ferrari.
3. Things you want your clothes to be made of: silk, wool, leather. Things you don't: polyester, cardboard, meat loaf.
4. A name on your clothing will impress people, provided it is something like Gucci, and not the name of your bowling team.

5. Wear red or black. These are powerful, commanding colors, often known to give noogies to weak colors like mauve and beige.
6. Check out what the models in the Paris fashion shows are wearing, and see that you don't make the same mistakes.
7. Think twice about any ensemble that includes plastic fruit.

Need I add that *how* you wear it is just as important as *what* you wear? A topcoat should always be draped over the shoulders, so some flunky can pluck it off. Sweaters should always be tied around the neck, so you never have to worry about about getting the right size. And underwear should always be worn *under* your clothes, so no one will see the little bears.

EGO WEAR

Wear one of the items listed below and you'll have a leg up on everyone else in the room. What the heck! Wear two! On you, *everything* looks good!

diamond tiara

sunglasses with mirrored lenses

Olympic gold medal

halo

pocket hot tub

bullhorn

ruby slippers

protective force field

field marshal's uniform

Mensa T-shirt

karate black belt

live snake

spacesuit

dueling scar

haughty expression

alligator shoes (with alligator attached)

tie signed by Picasso

Of course, if you *really* want to look superior, I suggest you wear something in basic orange and black. At least, it's always worked for me.

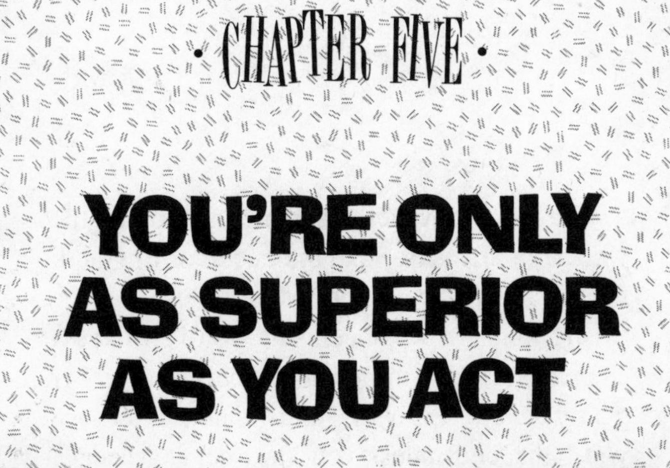

· CHAPTER FIVE ·

YOU'RE ONLY AS SUPERIOR AS YOU ACT

·ME·

You can always tell a superior person by the way he or she acts. Take the queen of England, for instance. If you met her on a bus, and she wasn't wearing her queen suit, you'd still know she was someone important by her bearing, her gestures, and the way she threatened to have you beheaded unless you gave her your seat.

Assuming that you've taken to heart every word that I've said so far, you now know how to feel superior and dress superior. So it's time you learned how to *act* superior. We'll start by discussing some superior expressions.

The Sneer: This look provides just the right mixture of arrogance and contempt. Lets the world know that *you* are cool, while virtually everyone else is something you scrape off your shoe. A must for teenagers.

The Eyeball Roll: Indicates that some thick-headed, exasperating lower life form is wasting your valuable time, but you have too much class to raise a stink about it. Very useful when traveling abroad.

The Brick Face: This is a look of total indifference, which says that you are perfectly aware of what's happening around you, but are too important to show the slightest interest in such trivia. Good expression to use on brothers-in-law, singing telegrams, special prosecutors.

The Crushing Smile: Used primarily when you are being introduced, this smile puts people in their place by saying, "The pleasure is all yours. Now, why don't you get back on the buffet with the other vegetables?"

LET YOUR BODY DO THE TALKING

There's more to acting superior than simple facial expressions. You also have to use your body to send those subtle, but unmistakable, messages of personal power. Here are some suggestions for using superior body language:

1. When sitting, the best way to exude authority is to sit upright with your legs uncrossed. This is especially effective if you are sitting on a

throne surrounded by armed bodyguards. If you don't have a throne, sit on the person you're talking to.

2. People equate height with authority, so you'll appear more powerful if you keep your head higher than the people with whom you are dealing. That's not always easy. In some cases you might need to staple yourself to the ceiling or bounce up and down on a trampoline. In any case, don't ever look up to people. If others have the height advantage over you, simply keep your gaze level, forcing *them* to bend down to make eye contact with you.

3. Gestures often speak louder than words. Clasping your hands together means you are serious. Clasping them around someone else's throat means you are very serious. You can also get an edge in conversation by poking the other person in the chest, preferably with a cattle prod. Other ways to intimidate people include staring until they look away, standing on their toes, and sticking your chewing gum to their forehead.

4. When in doubt, lie down. As far as I'm concerned, this is *always* a superior position.

· CHAPTER SIX ·

I'M IN CHARGE HERE

Wimps take life as it comes; superior people slap life up the side of the head until it gives them turf. If you want to be superior, you've got to be in command. With that in mind, here are my suggestions for taking control of certain situations by generally driving other people up the wall:

At a fancy restaurant

There are several ways to keep a haughty waiter off-balance:

— Keep a notebook open beside your plate. Let the waiter see you jotting down comments about the food and the service. If he asks about it, say, "It's just a little something for publication."

— Each time your waiter leaves your table, you and your companions should change places.

— Ask your waiter to recommend an appetizer or entrée. Whatever he recommends, say that a friend of yours ordered that once, and he was sick for a week.

At the dentist

— Eat plenty of onions and garlic before your appointment. This will keep your dentist from dawdling in your mouth.

— If you've never been to this dentist before, tell him/her that you hardly ever do that "biting thing" anymore.

— Ask your dentist if he/she read about that patient who went berserk and performed multiple extractions on his dentist. As you say this, stare at the instruments and breathe rapidly.

At the car dealer

— When you meet the salesman, don't tell him your correct first name. Wait till you're negotiating the price, then ask him why he's been calling you x when your name is y. Let him wonder if this little faux pas is going to blow the sale.

— Just before you close the deal, tell the salesperson that your first child was born in the back seat of your old car, and you don't think you can bear to part with it. A tear or two wouldn't hurt.

At your analyst

— When your analyst asks, "How are you today?" you should snap, "That's none of your business!"

— Tell your analyst that you've been having this strange dream every night. You can't remember all the details, but it involves the analyst, a Veg-o-Matic, and lots of screaming. Say you always wake up covered in sweat, but feeling strangely euphoric.

On a blind date

— When the door opens, look surprised and say, "Why, you don't look *at all* like a schnauzer!"

— Sometime during the date, mention that, if you could be anyone in the world, you'd be Freddy Krueger.

In the classroom

If you're a teacher . . .

— Give lots of pop quizzes. Give them on different days and at varying times, so your students will live in constant fear.

— Lecture while pacing back and forth on top of your desk. Using a bullhorn is a nice touch.

— Hire a classroom bouncer.

If you're a student . . .
— Write your quiz answers in Latin.
— Before class, inform your teacher that someone's science project has escaped and was last seen in the vicinity of the teacher's desk.
— Sit in the front row with a video camera pointed at your teacher. This should make him/her feel just a bit self-conscious.

At your IRS tax audit
— Start by telling the auditor not to blame himself/herself for "whatever happens."
— Be accompanied by two large men in dark suits, whom you should introduce as your "associates."

On the golf course
—Just as your partner is about to hit a crucial shot, make your beeper go off. Be sure you apologize for the "rotten timing."
—Watch your partner take a practice swing, then say, "I hate it when people advise me about my golf swing, so all I'm going to say is 'Think about your right hip.' " This should destroy your partner's swing for the rest of the round.

Okay, so I've told you all about putting your ego into action. What you need now is a little practice. Let's start by showing the refrigerator who's boss.

THERE'S A LOVELY VIEW AT THE TOP

Under the general heading of "Superiority" you'll find many different "Sub-Superiorities." For instance, there's "natural superiority," which means that cats are more intelligent, talented, and attractive than dogs and other vermin. Then there's "edible superiority," which means that lasagna is a better thing to put in your mouth than dirty sweat socks. Not to mention "catastrophic superiority," which means that being crushed by a falling meteor while fleeing a tidal wave is more traumatic than, say, getting a cold sore. But for the purposes of this

book, we need to concentrate on "personal superiority," which means that you are generally more intelligent, talented, and attractive than your average pro wrestling fan.

There are different types of personal superiority. So we ought to take a look at what your options are, and what advantages these different types of superiority have to offer:

Moral Superiority

Offers self-respect and the fun of knowing that you're good and most everyone else is a rock-worshipping heathen. Ability to cast out demons always a big hit at parties. Might get your own TV show. Tax breaks.

Intellectual Superiority

Allows you to wear tweed, solve crossword puzzles, actually read and understand poetry. Could be lifesaver if seated next to William F. Buckley on long plane ride.

Social Superiority

Get to look down on riffraff. Your name in the society columns. Country club dinners, debutante balls, polo at the Ritz. You never have to make your own bed.

Artistic Superiority

Means you can do any kind of garbage you want and call it "art." Might get to be on PBS. Bear in mind that true artistic superiority is not always recognized, though you could become extremely important about a hundred years after you starve to death.

Athletic Superiority

Offers wealth, fame, a tremendous sense of accomplishment, plus you get to snap towels at people. Plenty of free time to relax during off-season or while recovering from surgery. Good hand-eye coordination means you never stick your food up your nose.

Economic Superiority

Surely one of the best sub-superiorities, it speaks for itself. With enough money you can buy most of the sub-superiorities listed above. And you don't even have to wait till they're on sale.

As you can see, these types of superiority are all attractive in their own right, and achieving any one of them would be a feather in your ego.

But I haven't mentioned yet one of the prime types of personal superiority, and that's "job superiority."

Job superiority means having an enormous salary, numerous perks, and best of all, the power to make other people eat dirt. I'm talking about the really top-level positions here, jobs that are big enough for the biggest ego, like czar, king, or owner of the New York Yankees. Of course, people who hold these positions will tell you that they have to put in long hours, bear heavy responsibilities, and make gut-wrenching decisions. This is all true. What they don't tell you is that they do all these things from their yachts. Uneasy lies the head that wears a crown, but you don't see a lot of kings applying for the job of peasant, do you? Let's face it—it feels good to be boss. And the bigger the boss, the better the feeling.

Unfortunately, like all things worth having, job superiority is difficult to attain. And there's not a lot of room at the top. This means that most of you will never get to be the Big Boss. So be it. Your object should be to go as high as you can go, as fast as you can get there.

· CHAPTER EIGHT ·

GETTING YOUR EGO IN THE DOOR

Before you can become a ruthless chief executive, you must first become a ruthless job hunter. As a ruthless job hunter, your object will be to impress someone into hiring you. That means you will have to make a superior first impression, because first impressions are important and lasting. I speak from experience. I made a terrific first impression on myself, and I've never really gotten over it.

THE SUPERIOR RÉSUMÉ

If you, the job hunter, want to make a superior first impression, you will need to create a superior résumé. The superior résumé is vital to your success. A superior résumé gets noticed in a *good* i.e. "Let's hire this person" way, while an inferior résumé gets noticed in a *bad* i.e. "Let's slap this person" way.

Every superior résumé should include the following things:

personal information
educational background
work experience
salary requirements
references
bribe money

These are just the general headings, of course. With this as a guide, you create an impressive résumé by providing the appropriate information. Or *mis*information. Because the hard truth is that, even though you are obviously a superior person and are loved by your family and friends, on paper you may look like something of a geek. In that case, you will have to do a little creative résumé writing.

As an example, your education credits should be appropriate for the job you are seeking. If you are applying for a job as a brain surgeon, you are more likely to be hired if you say that you graduated from medical school. At the very least you should say that you got a passing grade in Health class.

The same thing holds true for work experience. You have to give them what they want to read. In most cases that means stating that you have experience in the specific job they are trying to fill. Don't be held back by the facts. So what if you don't really have three years experience as a "nuclear reactor operator"? You can operate a microwave oven, can't you? How much different can it be?

"Salary requirements" is a category that must be handled with great delicacy. Your first instinct, of course, is to write down "$1,000,000." You know you're worth that much, and if your employers had any insight, they would know it, too. Employers are not known for their insight, however, and only those employees who protect our vital national interests by playing sports ever get to make that kind of dough in an entry level position. So, when it comes to salary, you might want to plug one of these statements into your résumé:

"Negotiable."

"Just enough to get Mom that artificial heart."

"Whatever will allow me to give you a sizable kickback."

When it comes to references, the important thing is not just to list people who know you well. The important thing is to list people who know you well *and are willing to lie for you.* If you can't think of anyone who fits this description, then you should list people who know you well *and are deceased.*

DON'TS OF SUPERIOR RÉSUMÉ WRITING

Don't use crayon.

Don't look too good. People may not buy it if you say you have received a Nobel Prize. Say you almost got one, but it was lost in the mail.

Don't mention your fascination with lint.

Don't include a résumé for each of your personalities.

Don't write "Guess who?" in place of your name.

THE SUPERIOR INTERVIEW

Once your superior résumé has excited the proper interest, you will be called in for an interview. There's no need to be nervous about this. Remember, you are a superior person and can handle anything. "But," you say, "won't the interviewer ask questions that will reveal the creativity in my résumé?" By way of an answer,

let's peruse this transcript of a typical job interview involving a personnel manager (PM) and a job applicant (JA):

PM: How are you today?

JA: Fine, thanks.

PM: Any trouble finding this place?

JA: No, none at all.

PM: Have you ever beaned an old lady with a frozen carp?

JA: I don't think so.

PM: When can you start?

What does this mean for you, the job applicant? Basically it means that, since the interviewer really doesn't care, as long as you don't confess to being a mass murderer, the job is yours.

Speaking of jobs, this book is a lot of work. But if I can help just one person to stomp on the little guy, it will all be worth it.

· CHAPTER NINE ·

HOW TO SWIM WITH THE SHARKS AND EAT THEM

Let's assume that you have impressed/fooled/bribed someone into hiring you. Congratulations. You are now an inhabitant of the Working World. And what law governs the Working World? The law of the jungle. And what is the law of the jungle? Never, ever yell "Mice!" in a theater full of elephants. No, wait—that's not the law I meant. The law of the jungle is . . . survival of the fittest. Do you know what that means? It means that *you* have to stay on your toes, and *I* have to stay out of the jungle.

Once you've got a foothold on the company ladder, you should immediately begin clawing your way to the top. There are several ways to get there.

One of the best ways is to have your mother or father appoint you president of the company, preferably when you are about ten years old. This offers many advantages to a child, such as practical experience, accelerated maturity, and an accounting department to do your math homework.

The traditional way to the top is to rise through hard work, talent, and perseverance.

The only problem with this approach is that it requires hard work, talent, and perseverance. And there's no guarantee that your efforts will pay off. You can spend your entire career toiling faithfully, inching your way up the company ladder, only to walk into your office one day and find a ten-year-old sitting at your desk, telling Accounting to hurry it up with his math homework.

This leaves you with only one reasonable alternative, which is to claw your way to the top using every dirty, underhanded scheme you can

think of. Countless people throughout history have used this approach to get ahead. Genghis Khan, for example, became ruler of the Mongols by spreading vicious office gossip about his rivals. But I like to think of this approach as the "Garfield Method," because, after all, this book is about *me*.

LEARNING TO LIKE LACKEYS

Okay, it's time to start climbing. The first thing you need to do is recruit some lackeys. No one ever got to the top without lackeys. Without lackeys, Julius Caesar would have been just another guy in a sheet.

There are several reasons why you need lackeys:

1. In order to be "in charge," you need someone to be in charge *of.* That's where lackeys come in. They live to take orders.

2. You need lackeys to do the real work while you are thinking up new schemes for self-aggrandizement.

3. Lackeys don't mind taking the blame, especially if you threaten to expose them as thumb-suckers. Having a lackey to take the fall can be very comforting to you if one of your schemes goes awry.

So, get some lackeys. If you can't get lackeys, get flunkies. If you can't get good flunkies (and good flunkies are hard to find), see if you can at least scrape up a few snivelling bootlickers.

And how do you get lackeys? The best way is to start giving orders and see who actually carries them out. Most people will simply assume

you are an obnoxious jerk, and ignore you. But eventually you will find some not-terribly-bright person who will take you seriously. Embrace this person. Feed their low self-esteem with condescending remarks. And never let them see this book.

Another way to increase your pool of worker bees is to requisition them. After you've been on the job for a while, inform your boss that you need an assistant. Make it clear that having an assistant will allow you to do some of the boss's

work. Your boss will like that. Also, an assistant will allow you to do some much-needed special projects, which your boss can take credit for. In addition, your boss will become more important for having one more person, i.e. your assistant, under his command.

Naturally, all of your present duties, plus any new duties that look like real work, should immediately be dumped on your assistant. In this way your assistant will be overloaded with work in no time. Then you can ask your boss for an additional assistant.

JUST SAY "YES" TO BOSSES

Although it is patently obvious that you should be running the company, you will probably have to start in a subordinate position and work your way to the top. In the meantime you will be forced to deal with someone whose clout is cloutier than yours. I speak of your boss.

Your boss has a very important role to play in your career. Your boss must be a mentor, giving you advice, and providing you with information to use against others in the company. Your boss must shield you from the other little sharks, who would love to rip your fins off. Your boss must praise you to his/her bosses, speeding your promotions and raises. As you can see, your boss can do a lot for you. So you must be loyal to your boss. You must get him to like and trust you. That way it will be easier for you to take his job.

There are a number of ways to make points with your boss. Listed below are some of the best. Commit them to memory. You never know when you'll get the chance to suck up!

If you really want to impress your boss . . .

1. Be there in the morning when the boss arrives, and still be there when the boss leaves at night. Between times take a long lunch and catch a few winks.

2. Ask your boss to give you more work. Then dump it on someone else.

3. If your boss likes certain cookies or candies, keep a jar of them on your desk.

4. Ask your boss to recommend a restaurant. Have a "wonderful meal" there, whether you actually go or not.

5. Always say "thanks," even if *you* are the one who did the favor.

6. Ask to see pictures of your boss's family. Be complimentary, no matter how much you're reminded of the movie *Aliens.*

7. When your boss is talking, always pretend to listen.

Of course, if you *really, really* want to impress your boss, then you might consider trying one of these:

1. Go to the dentist for your boss.

2. Ask your boss if you can write his/her biography.

3. Name your child after your boss.

4. Give your boss a kidney. (If it's yours, so much the better.)

5. Swear that your boss's picture miraculously cured your split ends.

6. Fall on a grenade tossed at your boss.

7. Ask if you can take a cut in pay.

THE SUPERIOR OFFICE

So . . . the long hours of plotting have paid off, and you have been rewarded with your own office. Your office is a reflection of yourself, so naturally you will want it to be a superior office. In that case, this is what you'll need:

1. **Big desk.** Desk size is very important; it is a measure of your status in the company. The bigger your desk, the more power you have. John D. Rockefeller's desk was so big he had to take a limo just to reach the paper clips.

2. **Windows.** All superior offices have windows, preferably behind the desk. In this way you will be silhouetted against the light, forcing your visitors to squint, while giving yourself a certain god-like radiance.

3. **Computer.** You must have a computer to show that you are in touch with the latest technology. Plus, it's useful for playing computer games while your lackeys are working. You might want to learn how to turn it on and off, in case your secretary is sick.

4. **Phone with lots of buttons.** Powerful people get lots of phone calls from other powerful people who want to know what computer games they should get. Whenever your boss drops by, see that you are on the phone saying stuff like "I don't want excuses; I want results!" and "I'm sorry, but Mommy can't come home until she's boosted net earnings while trimming costs."

5. **Exercise machine.** This will show everyone that you are youthful, energetic, and dynamic—everything a powerful executive should be. Have someone dust it once a week.

6. **Calendar filled with appointments.** People will be impressed that you are so much in demand. And you can make a lot of points with someone if they think you are breaking another engagement just to meet with them.

7. **Visitor's chair which wobbles or squeaks.** This will distract your visitors, giving you an edge.

8. **Stack of trade magazines.** Shows that you are well-informed, plus you can have fun defacing the pictures.

9. **Wall filled with awards, plaques, keys to cities.** You can pick these up at flea markets, have the engraving changed. If asked, say you get so many, you can't remember what they're for.

10. **Document shredder.** You don't want incriminating evidence lying around, do you?

LET 'EM EAT SHARKBAIT

In the words of a great philosopher, "Life is a food chain, and it's better to be the diner than the dinner." I've always been impressed by the wisdom of that saying. But then, I'm impressed by everything I say.

The point is, if you want to get to the top, you're going to have to gobble up your competition (a.k.a. Sharkbait) along the way. To that end, here are some brilliantly cunning suggestions for turning rivals into fodder for your ambitions:

1. Invite your boss and Sharkbait to dinner, but tell Sharkbait the wrong day. When Sharkbait doesn't show, apologize to your boss, saying that Sharkbait sometimes has a little "spell."

2. Learn the ins and outs of the company audio-visual equipment. Then, before Sharkbait's presentation, discretely disconnect a wire or loosen a bulb. Let Sharkbait fumble for a moment, then step in and take command. It's amazing how competent you can look just changing a light bulb.

3. Circulate a memo, ostensibly from Sharkbait, suggesting that everyone work a half-day on Christmas. This will make Sharkbait *very* popular with the other employees.

LONG LIVE ME!

If you adhere faithfully to the "Garfield method" of business behavior, then someday you will become a top executive or even a precinct committeeman. Of course, once you've gotten to the top, you will be putting in a lot of long hours on your yacht figuring out the best way to *stay* on top. But that part is easy. You can pretty much be assured of keeping your cushy position if you simply follow these three rules:

1. Shift the blame.
2. Keep plenty of toilet paper in the company restrooms.
3. Never, ever hire anyone like yourself.

End of lesson.

Now that I've said all there is to say about superiority in the workplace, I guess I should admit that my own work experience is rather limited.

And let's keep it that way.

· CHAPTER TEN ·

CAN YOU SAY "CONDESCENDING?"

If you've been studying this handbook carefully, you should have a pretty good feeling about yourself by now. That's good. But remember, it's not enough just to think that *you* are superior. You've also got to be convinced that *everyone else* is *inferior.*

To that end, here are some suggestions for looking down on just about everybody. And if you happen to be included in any of these groups, bear in mind that superior people can always take a joke.

HOW TO TALK DOWN TO . . .

Lawyers: "Law is certainly a viable career, if you can't get into med school."

Teachers: "I wish *I* only had to work nine months out of the year."

Artists: "Society needs artists. I mean, those bare walls would be sooo tiresome."

Actors: "I could never do what you do. I'm just too well-adjusted."

Actors (TV): "Did you do any real acting before you got into television?"

Athletes: "It must be nice to extend your adolescence like that."

Debutantes: "You're so lucky. With your name and money you'll never have to worry about your looks."

Accountants: "I used to have an accountant. Then I got a calculator."

Doctors: "You do such important work, even if it does feed on the suffering of others."

Journalists: "I know that if you had the budget, you could be doing major news stories just like Geraldo."

Secretaries: "Hey, how about getting me some coffee?"

Politicians: "Does your mother know what you do for a living?"

Foreigners: "That funny accent of yours is perfectly charming."

Writers: "It's amazing how you can fill up all those pages."

Ad execs: "Eliminating bad breath is every bit as important as wiping out hunger and disease."

Car salesmen: "Are you between honest jobs?"

Auto workers: "Don't worry. Many people work on an assembly line and go on to lead normal lives."

Singers: "There's no way to ruin great songs like that."

Vice-presidents: "It must beat working for a living."

Plumbers: "Every time I flush I'm reminded of you."

Producers: "If you can't have talent, at least you can be around it."

Cartoonists: "Well, we can't all be physicists."

Physicists: "That pocket protector is really *you!*"

Dogs: "Some people find drooling very attractive."

Models: "If I had your looks, I wouldn't think either."

Pet owners: "Maybe I'll get a pet someday when no one else can stand me."

Librarians: "Dusting those books must take lots of training."

Disc jockeys: "I listened to you once."

Mechanics: "It's amazing how much of the grease you're able to wash off."

Farmers: "How's the dirt business?"

Cab drivers: "I can see how driving a cab would make you an authority on everything."

· CHAPTER ELEVEN ·

WHAT EVERY SUPERIOR PERSON SHOULD KNOW

·ME·

Back in ancient times—I mean, before television and ball-point pens — it was possible for a person to know everything there was to know. That's history. Today the aspiring know-it-all is faced with an enormous and ever-growing pile of data which would give most computers indigestion.

Fortunately, being a superior person doesn't mean you have to know it all. It means that you have to *act* like you know it all. And acting like you know it all requires very little brains, which is a break for those of you who have been moving your lips since page one.

Anyway, if someone starts conversing with you on a subject you know nothing about, do one or all of the following things:

1. Nod your head and go "Hmm." Every now and then throw in a "How true."

2. Change the subject. If someone is bending your ear about quantum mechanics, for example, say "That reminds me, have you tried the cheese puffs?" If they persist, try "All this talk about quantum mechanics sure gives me a taste for cheese puffs." Then run to the buffet.

3. Bluff your way along. If they catch you in a mistake, say "Oh, I thought you meant the *other* quantum mechanics!"

4. If you see no other way to avoid embarrassment, fake a heart attack.

Of course, this doesn't mean your head should be filled with nothing but pictures of yourself, enthralling as those may be. As a superior person, you have to know something about superior-type stuff. So read on, Macduff (which is an allusion to Shakespeare, who was the big playwright before Neil Simon came along).

EVERYTHING YOU NEED TO KNOW ABOUT . . .

ART

—Abstract paintings look "interesting" or "expressive," not "like something my sick parakeet brought up."

—No matter what the guy at the flea market says, that black velvet *Mona Lisa* is probably *not* the original.

—Whistler became famous for painting his mother, which worked out much better than his attempt to wallpaper her.

—Rembrandt was a painter, Rodin was a sculptor, Toulouse-Lautrec was short, and Dali was the guy everyone sang "hello" to.

OPERA

—Most operas are in some language other than English. This is because, when a tenor sings "This rash is driving me crazy!" it sounds a lot better in Italian.
—Characters in opera sing to each other, rather than talk, and they tend to repeat themselves. Simply asking the time can take up an entire act.
—*Carmen* is a famous opera. It includes the famous aria "I Want Your Hot Gypsy Love."
—The opera *Aïda* features real elephants. Most operas make do with a soprano.

SHAKESPEARE

—Every superior person should know at least one quote from Shakespeare. For example, "All the world's a stage" *(As You Like It)*. Or, "That's a shealed peascod" *(King Lear)*, which just slays them at parties. By the way, *As You Like It* is a comedy, while *King Lear* is a tragedy, especially if you haven't read it before the test.

—In the theater of Shakespeare's day all women's roles were actually performed by men or boys. This accounts for that somewhat puzzling moment where Romeo says, "Fair Juliet, methinks you need a shave."

—Speaking of Romeo and Juliet, every maniac worth his ego knows that "Wherefore art thou Romeo?" means "Why are you (named) Romeo?" and *not* "Where are you, Romeo?" No kidding.

—Some people assert that "Shakespeare's" plays were actually written by someone else, such as the Earl of Oxford or Cliff's Notes. Nonsense! Any boob can tell they were written by Elvis.

OTHER LITERARY STUFF

—Memorize the following authors and titles: Cervantes, *Don Quixote;* Melville, *Moby Dick;* Tolstoy, *War and Peace;* Joyce, *Ulysses.*

These books are classics, which means they are very good for impressing people and squashing large, hairy spiders.

— Dante wrote an epic poem called *The Divine Comedy.* There are hardly any laughs in the whole poem, however, except for canto 197, where St. Peter slips Satan the whoopee cushion.

— In the Middle Ages the common method for driving out demons was to assign them a book report on *Beowulf.*

— "Mark Twain" was really Samuel Clemens, "George Eliot" was really Mary Ann Evans, "George Orwell" was really Eric Blair, and Joyce Kilmer was really a guy. (Would I kid about stuff like this?)

BALLET

— In ballet the story is told entirely through dance, so movement must be used to express sentiments such as "love," "jealousy," and "UNNNNGH! My tutu is too tight!"
— Ballerinas strive to maintain an elegant thinness, but it's nothing a little "cheesecake therapy" couldn't cure. The principal female dancer of the company is called the "prima ballerina" or "the main stick."
— Nijinsky, Nureyev, and Baryshnikov are among the greatest male dancers of this century. Pavlova, Fonteyn, and Kirkland are among the greatest female dancers. All of them are renowned for their grace, their artistry, and their ability to look good in silly costumes.

— Tchaikovsky composed three of the world's best-known ballets: *Swan Lake, The Nutcracker,* and *Sleeping Beauty.* Ironically, Tchaikovsky rarely attended the ballet, preferring to stay home to watch "Bowling For Serfs."
— Remember, ballet is a classy art. Superior people do *not* show their appreciation by yelling "Nice buns!" at the performers.

WORLD HISTORY

5000 B.C. Ancient Mesopotamians get tired of primitive life-style, decide to invent civilization.

44 B.C. Julius Caesar assassinated in Roman Senate on Ides of March. His last words are "I came, I saw, I bit the big one."

476 A.D. Roman Empire falls. Scholars disagree on the reason for the fall, so if anyone asks your opinion, you can say almost anything. Personally, I think it was stress.

1215 English barons force King John to sign the Magna Carta, which states that no free man in England can be deprived of liberty or property except through process of law. The king resents having to sign this document, cancels "Baron Appreciation" Day.

1480 The Spanish Inquisition—the church court of Spain—is created to weed out heresy, and gains a reputation for exceptional cruelty. Prisoners are subjected to all forms of torture, including thumbscrews, the rack, and Julio Iglesias albums.

1492 Christopher Columbus discovers America. Columbus makes four voyages to the New World, on all of which he completely misses North America, while continuing to think China is just around the corner. And this guy gets his own holiday?

1775 American Revolution begins when British troops fire on Minutemen at Lexington and Concord. Colonists retaliate by putting shaving cream in King George's wig.

1812 Napoleon invades Russia. He captures Moscow, but is forced to turn back when the Moscow hotels will not accept his traveller's checks.

1929 Stock market crash plunges United States into severe economic slowdown called the "Great Depression." Think of it as a Monday that lasted ten years.

And let's not forget the most significant date in the history of this or any other planet: **June 19, 1978**. My birthday.

GEOGRAPHY

If you want to display a superior grasp of geography, this is all you have to know:

1. That the world is round. Even though it looks flat on the map, don't be fooled.
2. The names of three countries (not including Disney World).
3. The names of three state capitals. Extra credit for knowing North *and* South Dakota (North is Bismarck, South is Pierre).
4. The location of the nearest all-night pasta restaurant.
5. Your zip code.

LANGUAGE

—*Jejune* (rhymes with "maroon") is a superior word. It means "insubstantial" or "uninteresting," but few people know this, so you can use it any way you like, e.g. "Jejune weather we're having" or "Is that a piece of jejune stuck in your teeth?"

— Unsuperior words you should avoid:

bodacious	yo'	belch
reckon	toejam	ain't
gross	a-comin'	tractor pull
eksetera	a-(whatever)	
barf	nukyalur	

— Superior people do not dangle prepositions at the end of a sentence. Don't say "Where is he at?"; say "Where is he at, Bubba?"

—Superior people use French words and phrases, like "merci," "c'est la vie," or "Eez zees zee bathroom?" People think France must be a superior country, because everyone there can actually speak and understand French (even the kids!).

CONCLUSION

Well, I've taught you everything I know about thinking, dressing, speaking, acting, and scheming like a superior person. Don't worry if you can't absorb all of this wisdom in just one reading. Rome wasn't eaten in a day, you know. Consider this a reference book. Go back to it when you need to boost your ego or brush up on your back-stabbing. Just be careful that it doesn't fall into the wrong hands.

I've been watching you during the course of this book, and I like what I see. You have potential. You have an ego with an appetite. You want to go places. You want to become a corporate biggie or discover a cure for dogs. You're pompous, arrogant, erudite, egocentric, ruthless, unscrupulous, grasping, clawing, and the best thing ever to happen to a mirror!

**NOW GET OUT THERE
AND DOMINATE SOMETHING!**